the language of
love

Other books by Graham Cooke

Crafted Prayer
The Secret of a Powerful Inner Life
Developing Your Prophetic Gifting
A Divine Confrontation

the language of love

Hearing and speaking the language of God

being with God series

Graham Cooke

Chosen

Grand Rapids, Michigan

Published by Chosen Books
A division of Baker Publishing Group
P.O. Box 6287, Grand Rapids, MI 49516–6287
www.chosenbooks.com

Originally published under the title *The Language of Promise* by Sovereign
World Limited of Tonbridge, Kent, England

Printed in the United States of America

                    Library of Congress Cataloging-in-Publication Data
Cooke, Graham.
    [Language of promise]
    The language of love : hearing and speaking the language of God /
Graham Cooke.
        p. cm.
    ISBN 0-8007-9381-1 (pbk.)
    1. God—Worship and love. I. Title.

BV4817.C63 2004
248.4—dc22

                                                            2004050018

I dedicate this book to the members of Odyssey, the businessmen's spirituality group in California that I co-lead with my great friend Tim Dickerson.

Our times together have been a compelling mixture of grace, search for truth, impacting dialogue, friendship, laughter and good wine. Thanks!

Contents

Introduction

Jesus was getting used to operating under the critical eye of the Sadducees and Pharisees. He had encountered them many times in His ministry and had always used the beauty of God's truth to stay one step ahead of them. Today would be no different. The Pharisees had heard that Jesus had stumped the Sadducees, so one of the Pharisees, a lawyer, asked Him a loaded question: "Teacher, which is the great commandment in the law?"

Jesus's answer summed up the call on every Christian who has followed Him in the two thousand years since:

> "The first of all the commandments is: 'Hear, O Israel, the LORD our God, the LORD is one. And you shall love the LORD your God with all your heart, with all your soul, with all your mind, and with all your strength.' This is the first commandment. And

the second, like it, is this: 'You shall love your neighbor as yourself.' There is no other commandment greater than these."

Mark 12:29–31

Christianity can be boiled down into those two statements—our role in life is to love God and to love everyone with whom we come into contact.

Jesus has not asked us to do something He has not already done Himself. God always obeys His own word—He cannot go against His own decrees. He does not ask us to do something He would not do. We can therefore look at the first commandment and know He loves us with all His heart, all His soul, all His mind and all His strength.

Never doubt that you are absolutely and completely loved by God. You are His beloved. Your role in life is to receive that love, return it to Him and pass it along to everyone around you. It is a tough job, I know, but someone has to do it. Love Him with everything in you—it all belongs to Him, anyway. And love anyone you come into contact with, anyone within touching distance. It does not matter what you are doing, where you are going or whom you are meeting—you are called to love others. It is irrelevant whether they are Christian or pre-Christian; they are your neighbors and you are called to touch them with the love of God.

God has taken the lead in this. He has come to each of us and poured His love into our spirits: "I love you with all My heart, all My soul, all My mind and all My strength. Everything in Me is dedicated to loving you. I've poured this love into you and you're going to have the pleasure of giving it back to Me."

This is our greatest blessing—God loves us passionately.

the language of love

Love is a topic humans have explored, pondered, considered and written about for as long as we have been around. We have looked at it from almost every angle, and it is a common experiential ground for humanity—everyone understands the feeling of love. Many, however, have a distorted view of the power of love. They have tried to capture it without seeking out its origin, God.

The apostle John understood well where love originated: "We love because he first loved us" (1 John 4:19, NIV). Before we were saved, most of us were going through life completely oblivious to whom God really is. One day, suddenly and miraculously, God invaded our world, taking the initiative and reaching out to us in love. We responded by returning that love to Him and found ourselves walking in salvation.

The way we begin life in God is the same way life continues with Him. God took the initial step—He loved us first. He came looking for us, spoke to us, sent those weird people to share the Gospel with us. We looked at those people sent into our lives and thought, *Wow, they seem a bit out of step with the real world.* But there was something that drew us—God Himself.

Our relationship with God is sustained by the same force of love that birthed it. God does not stop taking the initiative the moment we are saved. He is continually our Lover, and we are continually His beloved. Our job is to be loved by God—only God can love God. He comes into our lives and fills them with hope, faith and love. That pure love does something inside of us, which we give back to Him.

> "Life is to be fortified by many friendships. To love and to be loved is the greatest happiness of existence."
> —Sydney Smith

God's language is love

God adores us because He wants our adoration. God loves us because He wants our love. God speaks to us by His love. This is the language we need to hear from the Lord so we can speak it back to Him. It is a glorious cycle—God takes the initiative by loving us, and we return that love to Him. God can say nothing without using this language of love.

What is true in the natural is also true by the Spirit. Isaiah described this beautifully:

> For as the heavens are higher than the earth,
> So are My ways higher than your ways
> And My thoughts than your thoughts.
>
> For as the rain and the snow come down from
>   heaven,
> And do not return there without watering the earth
> And making it bear and sprout,
> And furnishing seed to the sower and bread to the
>   eater;
> So will My word be which goes forth from My
>   mouth;
> It will not return to Me empty,
> Without accomplishing what I desire,
> And without succeeding in the matter for which I
>   sent it.
>
> Isaiah 55:9–11, NASB

God's promise is as inevitable as rain falling. His words water our lives, making us fruitful and productive. We return this blessing through our words of praise and thanksgiving, our testimonies and witness to His nature and also by our actions, which may bring glory to the Lord.

James puts it differently, but it is still the same theme:

> Every good thing given and every perfect gift is from above, coming down from the Father of lights, with whom there is no variation or shifting shadow.
> In the exercise of His will He brought us forth by the word of truth, so that we would be a kind of first fruits among His creatures.
>
> James 1:17–18, NASB

Everything good and right comes from a Father who never changes. His consistency and faithfulness are the bedrock of our ability to receive. They simply do not depend upon us! He is the origin, cause, motive and source of every gift. It will always be this way. He is the beginning and the ending for all of us, for all time. His passion is to make each of us a joyful carrier of His Word through His promises, so that we may enjoy the certainty of receiving His gifts and goodness.

Think of it. We are the first fruits of His huge

desire to have a people who represent His excellence. Our role in the earth is to proclaim the fact of God's outstanding goodness by living the life of promise He has set aside for us. All God's promises are yes! and amen! in Christ Jesus. Paul put it this way in his letter to the church in Rome:

WHO HAS FIRST GIVEN TO HIM THAT IT MIGHT BE PAID BACK TO HIM AGAIN?
For from Him and through Him and to Him are all things. To Him be the glory forever. Amen.
Romans 11:35–36, NASB

It is not possible for us to initiate anything to God. Paul asks who has ever given to God first. God initiates. We respond by receiving, and then we give back to God the very thing He gave us in the first place—from, through and to Him are all things. Everything He wants from us He gives to us.

This is amazing, wonderful, outrageous and mind-boggling! This means that when the Holy Spirit convicts me of something, He is also relaying the Father's willingness to supply what I lack. Therefore:

▶ Unable to pray? Conviction releases the promise that He will help us.

▶ Struggling with unclean thoughts? Conviction brings with it the promise of purity.

▶ Problems with doubt or unbelief? With conviction the Lord seeks to initiate faith.

Get the message? The promise releases the gift. Conviction seeks to reestablish the divine order. The Holy Spirit points out our needs and the provision at the same time. Conviction restores us to being open to the goodness of God.

We must see ourselves in that cycle in the manner the Father has declared. To live as part of His cycle of life we must understand that all of His language to us is full of promise to us. He delights to speak to us and our expectancy blesses Him.

The tragedy of modern Christianity is that much of it is performance oriented. We think we have to do something to get something from God: "God can't possibly like me because I'm not doing anything. God can't love me—I don't pray enough; I don't give enough; I don't worship enough; I don't read enough." But how much is enough? We shouldn't constantly be quantifying "enough," but we should be serving God because He loves us. Present-day Christians are quick to fall into the same trap Martha did in Luke 10, thinking we have to prove ourselves worthy of a relationship with Jesus. Being Mary and basking in Jesus' love is a severe challenge for us.

The language of love is something we must all learn. We have to understand how God sees us, so that we can see Him more clearly. God loves us, and because He loves us we want to talk to Him. Everything we can give to God comes from Him in the first place. It begins and ends with God, because intimacy is a cycle.

"Love is but the discovery of ourselves in others, and the delight in the recognition."
—Alexander Smith

In the natural world, we see many examples of this type of cycle. Water falls from the sky and returns to the heavens by the process of evaporation. The moon does not generate its own light but reflects the light of the sun in the night sky. The image in a mirror is nothing more than a reflection of the actual object. Likewise, our love for God is a reflection of His love for us. Love begins and ends with God.

We cannot love God on our own initiative, but we can give back that which He has bestowed on us. When the Father of Lights gives us a gift that touches our hearts, it does something inside us. We end up returning to God the very thing He has given us. To love God, we must be loved by God. It is a wonderful thing to go through our entire lives with God loving us. Our destiny is to have His love forever. We cannot escape it. We have no alternative but to put up with it—this is who God is.

Parents know an example of this principle. When our children were growing up, and our birthdays were approaching, most of us gave them money to buy us a present. How do we know how to do this? It is in our DNA. God is the same—His love is the currency He gives us so we can love Him more fully. He gives us the very thing He wants from us!

possessed by God

God chose us so He could be Himself with us. He wants us to see Him as He really is and to fall in love with Him the same way He has fallen in love with us. In our relationship, we must come to a place of mutual declaration, as He and the Israelites did:

> The LORD your God commands you this day to follow these decrees and laws; carefully observe them with all your heart and with all your soul. You have declared this day that the LORD is your God and that you will walk in his ways, that you will keep his decrees, commands and laws, and that you will

obey him. And the LORD has declared this day that you are his people, his treasured possession as he promised, and that you are to keep all his commands. He has declared that he will set you in praise, fame and honor high above all the nations he has made and that you will be a people holy to the LORD your God, as he promised.

Deuteronomy 26:16–19, NIV

God declared to the Israelites His laws, and the Israelites in return declared that they would follow God's laws. It was a breakthrough moment for the Israelites. Just outside the Promised Land with their leader, Moses, winding down his life, they finally came to a point of mutual declaration with God. This passage actually fulfilled a prophetic conversation Moses and God had shared forty years earlier:

And Moses went up to God, and the LORD called to him from the mountain, saying, "Thus you shall say to the house of Jacob, and tell the children of Israel: 'You have seen what I did to the Egyptians, and how I bore you on eagles' wings and brought you to Myself. Now therefore, if you will indeed obey My voice and keep My covenant, then you shall be a special treasure to Me above all people; for all the earth is Mine. And you shall be to Me a kingdom of

priests and a holy nation.' These are the words
which you shall speak to the children of Israel."

Exodus 19:3 – 6

Moses and Israel had been out of Egypt for just
three months when God spoke these words. The
words "special treasure" can also be interpreted as
"possession." "If you will indeed obey My voice and
keep My covenant, then you shall be *My possession*,"
God is saying. "The whole earth is Mine, but you will
be My special treasure." Those simple words began a
prophetic theme from the heart of God that has
echoed through countless generations.

This original prophetic blessing was later updated
and expanded:

> For you are a holy people to the LORD your God; the
> LORD your God has chosen you to be a people for
> Himself, a special treasure above all the peoples on
> the face of the earth. The LORD did not set His love
> on you nor choose you because you were more in
> number than any other people, for you were the
> least of all peoples; but because the LORD loves you,
> and because He would keep the oath which He
> swore to your fathers, the LORD has brought you out
> with a mighty hand, and redeemed you from the
> house of bondage, from the hand of Pharaoh king of

Egypt. Therefore know that the LORD your God, He is God, the faithful God who keeps covenant and mercy for a thousand generations with those who love Him and keep His commandments.

Deuteronomy 7:6–9

God has chosen us as His special treasure not because of who we are but because of who He is. His love cuts away all of our performance-oriented mentality. God chose us because of who He is; He chose us because of what He is like. We weren't chosen because we are deserving or clever or brilliant or handsome or noble or even good. He chose us because *He* is good. Out of His love and His promises we were selected as His treasure. God's faithfulness has been the bedrock of His dealings with humanity throughout time. God cannot change—He cannot be anything other than who He is.

> "Everybody can be great ... because anybody can serve. You don't have to have a college degree to serve. You don't have to make your subject and verb agree to serve. You only need a heart full of grace, a soul generated by love."
> —Dr. Martin Luther King Jr.

intimacy with God

Much of the terminology surrounding revival is geared to events and special circumstances. It is largely "visitation" terminology. We are looking for God to come in a move of the Spirit. Yet the language of Scripture is one of abiding, a habitation of the Spirit being built inside each of us.

In reality, revival is not about large numbers of people discovering the King and His Kingdom. Something spiritually dead cannot be revived—it must be born again. Revival is for the Church, not the world. We must wake up from our sleep.

Revival has three stages. First is renewal of our passion for Jesus. We must return to our first love and learn to abandon ourselves to His grace and power. Second, we must be revived in our compassion for the lost, to give our lives in service of the Kingdom. The outcome of these two initiatives will release a third and final stage—a reformation where the world will begin to respond to the power and the glory of a risen Lord, inhabiting His people.

We need to lay down our agendas and words and give ourselves day in and day out to loving Jesus, who taught, "He who believes in Me, as the Scripture has said, out of his heart will flow rivers of living water" (John 7:38). People all too often come to church meetings because they are thirsty. I just cannot understand that. We should be coming to meetings because we are full of water and want to give more of it away.

Learning to live with God takes time. The pressure of ministry is intense. It can stress us, make us sick, even kill us, unless we know how to rest in the Lord. It takes discipline to bring ourselves to a place of peace before God, but it is absolutely necessary to do so. It has taken years of practice for me, but on most days I can bring myself to that place of peace in five or ten seconds. It no longer matters what is swirling around me or threatening me; I can still myself before God. I have to, for I need to be quiet to hear His voice. God loves to speak in whispers— He rarely answers prayers at the same decibel level at which they are prayed.

"Father!" we shout. "I need to hear Your voice!"

"I know," He whispers back.

"Speak to me!"

"I am," He whispers.

"I need to hear Your voice today!"

"Be quiet and listen," He whispers.

"Be still, and know that I am God," says Psalm 46:10, NKJV. Meditation is another avenue toward intimacy with God. The western Church must learn to meditate, setting time aside to think deeply about God. It does not have to be long, just fifteen minutes or half an hour, but the more you do it the more time you'll want to give to Him. I love meditating.

Meditation and stillness flow into an upgrade of our peace. I spend a lot of time on peace with the people I disciple. I constantly confront them on the issue of peace in their lives. I do not expect them to worry or panic at the same level next year as they did this year. Their peace must increase and anxiety decrease. Peace is a vital fruit of the Spirit.

Without an upgrade in our capacity to rest in the Lord, we find ourselves running on adrenaline. That is okay for a while, but for every adrenaline high, there is an adrenaline low. Often people get down and depressed because they have been running on adrenaline, and they have run out. It is not the pressure of life that gets to us; it is the pressure of how we run it.

Peace, though, is an equalizing pressure. If the world is throwing a thousand pounds of pressure at us from the outside, peace sends a thousand and one pounds from the inside. I am under pressure wherever I go—intense pressure in most places. Everyone wants to see me and talk to me and pull at me and get prayer from me. I do not mind—it is my job. To survive, I

> "If the world is throwing a thousand pounds of pressure at us from the outside, peace sends a thousand and one pounds from the inside."

have learned to be at peace. My rest in God gives me space.

Eventually, adrenaline will rob our minds and bodies and leave us exhausted. It is okay to be tired *in* the work, but it is not okay to be tired *of* the work. We must learn to give ourselves to peace, rest and meditation. We can operate at the highest level for many years if we have developed ourselves internally in preparation.

sonship and stewardship

We live our lives in the tension of a paradox between *being* and *doing*. The key to succeeding in this quandary is always to choose *being* over *doing*. We must choose to take time out to rest. We all have to do many things, but being is just as important. This paradox could be described as the difference between *sonship* and *stewardship*. We must learn how to serve the Lord, but we must also explore how to be a son of God. God does not want to treat you like a slave—He wants to treat you like a son.

One of my mentors, Arthur, once asked me, "Graham, do you want to be a servant of the Lord?"

"Yes," I answered.

"Then don't get upset if He treats you like one," Arthur said.

Sometimes, God commands and I obey. Other times, He makes a request of me because He wants to treat me like His son. A Christian needs to know how to live life as both a servant and a son. Being a son means God gets the best of our day, not just the tail end. The apostle Paul is a wonderful example of a man who knew how to be both a servant and a son:

> Therefore I also, after I heard of your faith in the Lord Jesus and your love for all the saints, do not cease to give thanks for you, making mention of you in my prayers: that the God of our Lord Jesus Christ, the Father of glory, may give to you the spirit of wisdom and revelation in the knowledge of Him, the eyes of your understanding being enlightened; that you may know what is the hope of His calling, what are the riches of the glory of His inheritance in the saints, and what is the exceeding greatness of His power toward us who believe, according to the working of His mighty power which He worked in Christ when He raised Him from the dead and seated Him at His right hand in the heavenly places, far above all principality and power and might and dominion, and every name

that is named, not only in this age but also in that
which is to come.

And He put all things under His feet, and gave
Him to be head over all things to the church, which
is His body, the fullness of Him who fills all in all.

Ephesians 1:15–23

What an incredible prayer! Longevity in the spirit is
powered by wisdom and revelation from God. The
two streams flow into one, enabling us to
understand whom God wants to be for us. Once we
capture whom God wants to be for us, a power and
energy flows into our spirits from His own.
Suddenly, we are living life for all it is worth.
Defeats and burnout evaporate. A Spirit-infused
Christian does not become weary or overwhelmed by
circumstances, because his or her eyes are lightened
with the knowledge of who God is.
His call on our lives is certain.

Living in the Spirit gives us a
glimpse of the riches of our
inheritance. God loves to show us His
majesty and power so that in every
situation we face we know we can rely on Him. "I
know whom I have believed and am persuaded that
He is able to keep what I have committed to Him,"

> "Two roads diverged in a
> wood, and I ... I took the
> one less traveled by, and that
> has made all the difference."
> —Robert Frost

Paul writes to Timothy, his young charge (2 Timothy 1:12). He had absolute confidence in whom God was for him—his deliverer, his protector, his passion. Paul was able to go into places where incredible opposition swirled because he knew God was with him. He was always himself and spoke the words of God to kings and vagabonds.

Each of us can go only as far as God has given us permission to go. Our authority grows as our maturity in Christ grows. By knowing who God is for us we never have to be afraid of our circumstances.

lessons from Ephesus and two women

The paradox of being and doing is seen throughout Scripture. In the book of Revelation, we see one example of this phenomenon in a letter written by Christ to the church at Ephesus:

> To the angel of the church of Ephesus write,
> "These things says He who holds the seven stars in His right hand, who walks in the midst of the seven golden lampstands: 'I know your works, your labor, your patience, and that you cannot bear those who are evil. And you have tested those who say

they are apostles and are not, and have found them liars; and you have persevered and have patience, and have labored for My name's sake and have not become weary. Nevertheless I have this against you, that you have left your first love. Remember therefore from where you have fallen; repent and do the first works, or else I will come to you quickly and remove your lampstand from its place—unless you repent.' "

Revelation 2:1–5

The church of Ephesus was full of good, hardworking people. They loved to *do* ministry. Their church endured and persevered through troubles. They were efficient and did good deeds. Yet somehow their relationship with God had been lost in all of the business. "I have this against you, that you have left your first love," Jesus said. "Remember therefore from where you have fallen; repent and do the first works." In other words, God was calling Ephesus to think back to its acts of adoration and to reconnect with Him in worship.

Repentance means to change one's mind and find a different paradigm to live under. Ephesus, and by extension all Christians who *do* more than *be*, needed to change its lifestyle to reflect its most urgent priority—worshiping God. "Do the first works"—start by practicing all of the things you used to do in praise, in worship and in your devotional life.

God does not need people to evangelize the earth, do missions projects or give away millions of dollars. He looks for people who will worship Him in spirit and in truth. That does not just mean singing in meetings or going for it when the band is rocking. He wants people who worship Him in the way they live. He wants people like Mary and Martha:

> Now it happened as they went that He entered a certain village; and a certain woman named Martha welcomed Him into her house. And she had a sister called Mary, who also sat at Jesus' feet and heard His word. But Martha was distracted with much serving, and she approached Him and said, "Lord, do You not care that my sister has left me to serve alone? Therefore tell her to help me."
>
> And Jesus answered and said to her, "Martha, Martha, you are worried and troubled about many things. But one thing is needed, and Mary has chosen that good part, which will not be taken away from her."
>
> Luke 10:38–42

Both Mary and Martha were right, but for completely different reasons. Paradoxes are not about one right answer and one wrong one—both sides of a paradox are right. The issue is primacy. When push comes to shove, what is most important to us? What takes precedence? Without Marthas, very little would get done in the Church. Marthas sacrifice, organize and create places where Marys can flourish in worship. But without Marys, everything we do would come from a religious duty. We actually need both. Each of us is a Mary and a Martha, and both are legitimate. But one has precedence—Mary. Mary is where we receive insight into the things God has placed inside us.

> "Each of us is a Mary and a Martha, and both are legitimate."

Jesus Christ: treasure hunter

Throughout His earthly ministry, Jesus spoke to the treasure God had deposited in people. He even blessed the spiritual treasure people themselves did not realize they had. Jesus once met a crooked tax collector named Zacchaeus. Not once did Jesus reveal the man's sin. All He did was bless him and honor him. Humbled, Zacchaeus knew what to do:

"Look, Lord, I give half of my goods to the poor; and if I have taken anything from anyone by false accusation, I restore fourfold" (Luke 19:8). The man simply stopped cheating others, signed away half his possessions and made a contract with heaven to restore what he had previously stolen. "I robbed you of a hundred dollars; here's four hundred back." That is God at work in one of His special treasures.

God has placed His fingerprint in the people around us, and we need to speak to that spiritual treasure. In John's gospel we read that the disciple Philip brought his brother, Nathanael, to meet Jesus. Nathanael was at first skeptical: "Can anything good come out of Nazareth?" he asked. But when he finally met Jesus, the Lord spoke to the treasure in him: "Behold, an Israelite indeed, in whom is no deceit!" Jesus said, noting prophetically that He had seen Nathanael sitting under a fig tree earlier that day (John 1:46–48). "Rabbi, You are the Son of God! You are the King of Israel!" exclaimed Nathanael (John 1:49), who then left everything behind and became a disciple. Jesus had spotted the treasure deposited in Nathanael's life and had spoken to it. The result? Nathanael became a pillar of the early Church.

speak to the treasure

Jesus knew that whatever He spoke to would create greater value in people. Humanity always speaks to the earthen vessel, noting every crack, flaw and warp: "If you put this right, and change that, then we'll let you in and accept you." God is not remotely like that. He speaks to the treasure in a person and releases it from the captivity of the flesh. He extracts the precious from the worthless. We often try to do the opposite—take out the trash and see what is left. When we speak to the treasure in people, it moves to the surface of their lives, from the hidden to the obvious. And the rubbish always comes with it. When people see their own worth, they get rid of their own carnality. That is why the prophetic and the pastoral go so well together. But God knows there is treasure in each of us, and He wants to bring it to the surface. Do not let your view of the worthless obscure that which is precious about a person.

We have to change the way we think of and behave around other people. We must realize that our real enemies are the devil and his demons. The apostle Paul believed this: "For we do not wrestle against flesh and blood, but against principalities, against powers, against the rulers of the darkness of this age, against spiritual hosts of wickedness in the heavenly places" (Ephesians 6:12). Other people in whom we find no treasure are not our enemies. Fortunately, God can give us a different type of vision to help us see people in a new way, the way God sees us.

The apostle Peter wrote, "Let it be the hidden person of the heart, with the incorruptible beauty of a gentle and quiet spirit, which is very precious in the sight of God" (1 Peter 3:4). "Incorruptible" in this verse means the beauty will not pass away; unlike a flower that blooms and withers, that which is precious in God's eyes stands forever. When God looks at us, He see what is precious, what He loves most about us right now.

> "I have found the paradox that if I love until it hurts, then there is no hurt, but only more love."
> —Mother Teresa

love your enemy

Christians are quick to demonize other believers. Unfortunately, I have witnessed many examples of this fact. I remember talking with a well-known church leader whose associate pastor, after many years, had left and started another church five miles down the road.

"I discipled this guy for fifteen years and he went and left me!" the leader told me. "He's got an Absalom spirit!"

"What does that look like?" I asked.

"You know, Absalom. He's a traitor," the leader replied. "He's taken what is mine and seized it for himself."

I was surprised by the conversation. "I know that man," I said. "And the truth is that he can only be an Absalom if you have been a David. If you have been fatherly to him, kingly, looked after him, loved him and wanted only to see him succeed, then, yes, he is an Absalom. But if you haven't done that, he can't be an Absalom."

After a few moments of silence, I continued. "You know what, he might be a Jacob and you might be a Laban. Did you ever think about that? It works both ways."

He frowned at me, but I pressed ahead. "You're not seeing things clearly," I said. "Maybe you have forgotten all of the years that he served you. Maybe you have forgotten his faithfulness, like the time the church was having financial troubles, and he took a pay cut so you wouldn't have to. Maybe you have forgotten to see what God has put inside of him. Maybe he just feels that he has only one life and he

You See

I see a mountain, you see a miracle
I see a wasteland, you see a garden
I see dry bones, you see an army
I see the impossible, you see everything

I see a seed, you see a harvest
I see the water, you see the wine
I see the broken, you see your body
I see my enemy, you see your footstool

> You are, I am
> But I've been so blind, all this time
> My God, touch me
> I want to see the way that you see

I see my sins, you see your blood
I see a baby, you see my Savior
I see my failures, you see redemption
I see a beggar, you see a son

I see a problem, you see a provision
I see a circus, you see an opportunity
I see the image, you see the heart
I see opposition, you see someone to love

> You are, I am
> But I've been so blind, all this time
> My God, touch me
> I want to see the way that you see

I see the weary, you see the warriors
I see the restless, you see their peace
I see the doubting, you see their faith
I see the weak, you see their strength

I see my Father, you see your son
I see my Shepherd, you see your lamb
I see my Savior, you see your joy
I see your eyes, staring into mine

You are, I am
But I've been so blind, all this time
My God, touch me
I want to see the way that you see

Inspired by the lyrics of Jonathon Helser,
a songwriter, worshiper, catalyst and
man after God's own heart.

needs to live it. You got so used to him serving you that you forgot to serve him. You're a good man, and you can see this for yourself. In your heart, you are a father, and you've just missed that point for a few moments. Why don't you go down the road and say to him, 'How can I help you be successful?' You could lend him some of your people for a while, or see if he is okay financially. You might want to get behind him on some evangelistic initiatives just to bless him. Maybe you could just let him know that even though he has a problem or two, you see the good in him. Knowing you, you'll probably want to do all of this and more, because you are a godly guy."

> "Hatred paralyzes life; love releases it. Hatred confuses life; love harmonizes it. Hatred darkens life; love illumines it."
> —Dr. Martin Luther King Jr.

The leader paused and looked at me. "Do you want a coffee?" he asked. I got the message—subject closed.

Some time later, the former associate called me and told me that he and the leader had gotten together for coffee. The leader had apologized and had begun paying half the man's salary and had sent teams to help him with the church plant.

"What happened?" the former associate asked me, completely bewildered.

"I think he just saw the treasure in you, because God showed him the treasure inside himself," I answered.

start with yourself

Sometimes it is not the quality of people's sonship but our fathering that is more the issue. It is not just their commitment to service but also our capacity to inspire and disciple. These things always work both ways. First getting God's perspective enables us to position our own hearts in the Spirit.

The leader I mentioned earlier had to have a vision of himself—that he was a father, not a slave-owner—before he could have eyes to see the treasure in someone else. When we see ourselves as God sees us, we automatically start seeing others differently. I look at some people and think, *It's in there somewhere—just keep looking, Grae.* I want to love people enough to tell them what their treasures are. I do not want to focus on what they are doing against me. I want to come back, in the opposite spirit, and say, "You know something? This is what God likes about you."

This approach confounds people, and it is amazing to see it in action. People come to me and say, "I don't like this about you, or this, or this." I just smile, look at them and reply, "You're probably right, because I am less than perfect. But you know, this is what God likes about you. God loves this part of you! Let me just bless that in you, so you can get stronger." It is called heaping coals of fire on their heads, and it is a lot of fun. They usually leave bewildered by the conversation but touched by the Spirit.

Some of us have had our minds so damaged by others that we simply believe we are worthless. I curse that thought in the name of Jesus—that is not God. We should each know our value and worth to the Lord. It is not based on what we have done but on who He is. Our doings will catch up with our beings—do not fret about that. But God loves you, right now, just as you are. He will continue to change and form you, because He is kind, generous and in love with you.

In the Bible, God compared us with pure gold:

> The precious sons of Zion,
> Valuable as fine gold,
> How they are regarded as clay pots,
> The work of the hands of the potter!
>
> Lamentations 4:2

People see us as just another clay pot, made by a potter's hand, but God sees us as fine gold. Sometimes we cannot see the spiritual beauty in a person because of the earthen vessel, but the beauty is there. And whatever you see in people that is good, or speak to people that is good, rebounds on you. God judges every idle word and blesses every precious one.

> "God loves you, right now, just as you are."

what we are and what we are not

Everything we do is both an *act of worship* and an *act of war.* A good day's work is an act of worship because it demonstrates something about the Kingdom of God. It is also an act of war because the enemy hates employment. Spending time with God is a powerful act of worship and a terrifying act of war—our intimacy with the Lord intimidates the demonic. Every word of praise, every word of thanksgiving and every thought of adoration is a salvo in the battle against evil.

The enemy hates thankful people and enjoys misery. He loves grief, sadness, unhappiness, low self-esteem and anything that keeps a human from connecting with God. The Spirit of Christ is put into humans to ward those feelings off—God wants us to know how He feels about us. In that knowledge, He then wants us to reach out and take the grave clothes off the people around us. Everything positive and good is a spirit contribution that attacks death and decay, bringing light, hope and warmth into someone's heart.

My personality has never lent itself well to the stage. I am very much an introvert, so what you see in my preaching is completely fueled by God's anointing. I love the way God made me. Andreas Hermann, a German friend of mine, once said that "introverts have a very colorful inner life." He was absolutely correct—I do have a colorful inner life.

The downside of being introverted is that I get overwhelmed by myself some days. Waves of thoughts about what I am not crash over me, leaving me overwhelmed. Those thoughts are easily overcome, however. I need only think of how God feels about me, His love and adoration and kindness for me, and those worried thoughts dissipate. I am not fooled by myself. I know what I am like without Jesus, but I also know what my potential in Him is.

The apostle Paul wrote,

> And He said to me, "My grace is sufficient for you, for My strength is made perfect in weakness." Therefore most gladly I will rather boast in my infirmities, that the power of Christ may rest upon me. Therefore I take pleasure in infirmities, in reproaches, in needs, in persecutions, in distresses, for Christ's sake. For when I am weak, then I am strong.
>
> 2 Corinthians 12:9–10

Christians can look at God and thank Him for their deficiencies, for He covers all those weaknesses.

It is okay to come to God and say, "I don't deserve to be here. I am only here by Your grace, Your goodness, Your mercy and Your overwhelming kindness." I often tell the Lord that I do not know why He chose me, except that He must be looking for someone slow and degenerate. I fit that bill! All Christians live their lives by the grace of God. Our deficiencies are more than made up for by the Holy Spirit. God can and will make up the shortfall in our lives. God stands in our credibility gap and smiles. He stands in our hypocrisy and gives us legitimacy. And He does it gladly!

God calls each of us as a Jacob and makes us an Israel. This is the transition all of us will work through every day of our lives. In that space between Jacob and Israel stands Jesus Himself, loving us and offering us His credibility. This love is why Christians should be the most grateful people on the face of the earth.

"Only believe."
—Smith Wigglesworth

We need to return to the right spiritual disciplines because our primary goal must be to remain in the presence of God. We need to believe in the power and ministry of the Holy Spirit to sustain a devotional lifestyle. These disciplines—blessing, prayer, meditation, peace, rest, worship, thanksgiving and praise—are God's language of promise.

The Holy Spirit is committed to seeing us connect with God no matter what state our lives are in. His job is to help us find and enjoy the grace of God. The Lord loved us when He saw the worst we had ever been. In fact, what we are not endears us to Him. God came and chose and loved us in the midst of all of our sin, hypocrisy, inadequacy and inability. And as He works in our lives, our ability to experience that nonnegotiable love is increasing. His love never changes, but the way we receive it does. It is we who grow, not Him.

To our minds, it seems like God loves us more now than He did before. This is untrue. What has changed is that we believed His love, say, 10 percent back then, and we believe it 23 percent now. Next year, we might believe 45 percent of His love. Eventually, we are going to believe all the love God has for us. At that moment, nothing on earth will be able to stop us from becoming the people God has called us to be. Through the leading of the Holy Spirit, our confidence and faith in the nature of God can enable us to believe fully in the enormity of His love for us.

bless, bless and bless some more

If we were really sensible, we would be out there blessing up a storm, because every blessing we give someone returns to us. I write, on average, twenty cards a week. (I should have bought shares in Hallmark!) I will sit and think about people and ask the Lord to tell me something about them. God then shows me something precious and I write. Sometimes, it is just a few sentences: "I was thinking about you today, and this is what the Lord told me about you. Just thought you might want to know."

I do this, and it seems to returns to me tenfold. I remember being at home one day when Carole, my personal assistant, called to ask how I was doing.

> "The love we give away is the only love we keep."
> —Elbert Hubbard

"Really good," I answered.

She laughed and said, "Well, Graham, we've got 35 cards in the office for you. Are you sure you're not struggling with anything?"

"Actually, yes, I am struggling with something," I sighed. "I've been praying for it, but I don't know how I feel about it. I'm on the edge of it. I still feel good about myself, but something's up." I went to the office and read the 35 cards—and 27 of them spoke encouragement in the very issue I was facing.

You cannot sow potatoes and reap rhubarb. To be blessed and encouraged, we must bless and encourage others.

living by faith

I am never in need of encouragement or money because all I want to do is give both away. I have learned to hold on to both loosely, living by faith. I do not have a salary; I prefer to live by faith.

My struggles to live by faith early on in the ministry were centered mainly around my inability to rest. I had not worked out that the Father not only provides but also stretches our faith at the same time. That often meant the provision was delayed (my terminology) or at least never showed up when I was at the limit of my faith. It seems that God disagreed about where my limit was, however, and so each situation took me beyond my previous measure.

In the gap between promise and provision, I was slowly learning I had choices to make. Either I could rest in God's language of promise ("My God shall supply all your need in Christ Jesus") or I could try to make things happen by dropping hints to people, sending out prayer letters, expending my own efforts. Often in that hiatus I would get irritable and impatient with people around me, usually my wife, Heather.

I was not only learning about faith and how it grows by stretching, I was also discovering that faith must be undergirded by peace. The author of the letter to the Hebrews unites faith and rest: "We who have believed enter that rest" (Hebrews 4:3, NASB).

Hebrews speaks of laboring to enter a place of peace and calmness. Rest has to be worked at constantly or faith will whither. All Christians must increase their peace levels to be able to stay in the war, live the life and move in the supernatural.

Our faith is in the nature of God—it is not about faith in faith. So often I have heard people say they do not have enough faith. It is not the size of our faith that is important but the depth of our revelation of God's nature. When we know what He is really like, when our hearts are emboldened by the majesty of His faithfulness and grace, then we know His commitment to His word and His people cannot be broken. His word will not return to Him empty.

Faith is driven by what we have seen, heard and experienced of the true nature of the Father. Our faith always pushes out beyond our experience;

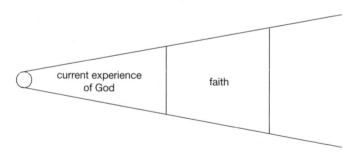

Figure 1

it never stays at the same place. Our current experience helps us to believe God more at the next opportunity (see figure 1). That is what Scripture means when it says we walk by faith, not sight.

There is always a dimension beyond our experience that faith is exploring, pushing us beyond the boundaries of what we know in the nature of God. As we get used to that faith level, our experience pushes up to it and our faith ranges out further into the heart of God (figure 2).

Our faith is always in advance of our experience, so that we always have something to aim for in the nature of God. In the storm on the lake (see Mark 4), the disciples had faith in their own seamanship but not in Jesus' power to control the elements. Faith gave out and fear came in as a result. The size of faith is always a lesser issue than where it is placed.

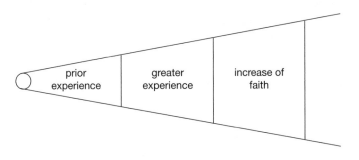

Figure 2

Shoes

My child, walk in My footsteps, live in My shoes.
This is your place of safety because I am bigger than anything
  or anyone you will ever face.

This is your place of provision, for you will walk in My increase
  for your life.
This is your place of expansion for I am growing you to fit the
  anointing that I have set aside for you.

You have power to stand in Me.
My strength is yours as you walk in Me.
Walking in bloody footsteps, your sins are forgiven and your
  weaknesses are covered.

Enjoy this life.
Be a child in Me.
Speak to your enemy, your detractors, your problems with the
  same confident word:
"My God is bigger that you."

It will always and ever be True!

real prosperity

In Acts we read of the apostle Peter's vision, which changed the course of Church history:

> The next day, as they went on their journey and drew near the city, Peter went up on the housetop to pray, about the sixth hour. Then he became very hungry and wanted to eat; but while they made ready, he fell into a trance and saw heaven opened and an object like a great sheet bound at the four corners, descending to him and let down to the earth. In it were all kinds of four-footed animals of the earth, wild beasts, creeping things, and birds of the air. And a voice came to him, "Rise, Peter; kill and eat."
>
> But Peter said, "Not so, Lord! For I have never eaten anything common or unclean."
>
> And a voice spoke to him again the second time, "What God has cleansed you must not call common." This was done three times. And the object was taken up into heaven again.
>
> Acts 10:9-16

God wanted Peter to see people the way He sees them—as precious treasures. "Don't call them dirty, Peter—I love them." The real prosperity message is

"Christ in you, the hope of glory" (Colossians 1:27). We must look for Jesus in the people around us.

God has sent us on a treasure hunt to find what He has implanted in people.

> "Love in its essence is spiritual fire."
> —Emanuel Swedenborg

In the beginning, God said, "Let Us make man in Our image, according to Our likeness" (Genesis 1:26). We must search for the image of God in every human being, looking for what is precious in Christian and pre-Christian alike.

a devotional lifestyle

Our search for the treasure in other people is just one part of the devotional lifestyle needed to free our ministries from stress and worry.

One of my earliest mentors once said to me, "You have to be in ministry for about 20 or 25 years before God will trust you with your life's message. In the first 20 years, everything is training and preparation for what God truly wants you to do." That is why longevity is so important in ministry. We must learn to live in a place where we can run without growing tired. We have to replenish ourselves in the Spirit every day.

Successful ministers plan for the future but live for today. They place their lives in day-tight compartments, taking everything one day at a time. At the end of a day, such ministers know how to shrug everything off, cleanse their hearts and minds and be thankful for the blessings God has given them. When they awake the next morning, they awake anew to the tangible mercies of God. Those mercies are like a first cup of coffee or a first mouthful of food.

When I first started out in prophetic ministry thirty years ago, although there were possibly many prophetic ministers in the UK, as far as I was aware there were just six of us—and three of these seemed strange. Ministry is relentless on people:

► a quarter of all prophets have nervous breakdowns
► 60 percent of all pastors quit leading churches
► 50 percent of people leaving the ministry do so because of immorality
► another 30 percent leave because of stress

Behind most of these statistics is a rundown devotional life. When we lose our focus on God, we end up with a working relationship but a lousy friendship with Him. The only way a lot of ministers relate to God is on the basis of what they do for Him. Everything is businesslike when people have lost their devotional lives. They end up praying about ministry—the youth group, Sunday School, finances and so on—and activity rather than the joy of friendship with the Father consumes them.

> "We have become so engrossed in the work of the Lord that we have forgotten the Lord of the work."
> —A. W. Tozer

I wonder how many of us have upgraded our abilities to praise and thank God in the past twelve months. We need to praise God more this year than we did last year. Many of us take time out every day to pray, but how many of us take time just to adore Jesus? A few questions will help us get to the heart of the matter:

► What attracts you to Jesus?
► What draws you to Him?
► What aspect of His nature overwhelms you in His presence?
► What is the most important thing for you to recover in your relationship with God?
► What gift does the Lord long to give you?

idolatry

A sixth question could be added to that list:

▶ What distracts you from enjoying the presence of God?

Martha was pulled away from Jesus' presence by her sense of duty and by the work necessary to house a guest of Jesus' stature. What interests you most has taken a piece of your heart. If the combination of people and things in your heart is greater than your love for God, your spirituality will hit a ceiling and level off. Often we do not know where God is in our lives because we have not given Him much room to move. The clutter of our other loves and desires, legitimate though some may be, can prevent His reality from being expressed. In extreme cases, they can even shut Him out altogether.

Many Christians are lukewarm in their fellowship with the Lord because the balance of their love and attention is swung away from the Father. Idolatry has such a beginning.

God's love raises the water table of all our other affections—it is as if our love for others comes up ten levels because of how we feel about Him. When

God rules out of our absolute love for Him, all other loves improve and increase.

Whatever comes between God and us is an idol. Whether it is our leadership, career, business, ministry, family or anything else, it is an idol. At that point, we are headed for either a pruning or a serious chastisement because God is a jealous God. He will not have anything come between Him and His children. Take some time and make sure your life is in proportion.

> "Without worship, we go about miserable."
> —A. W. Tozer

Jesus' words to the church in Ephesus need to ring loud and clear in our spirits: "Remember therefore from where you have fallen; repent and do the first works, or else I will come to you quickly and remove your lampstand from its place—unless you repent" (Revelation 2:5). The lampstand represents the place of revelation, influence and ministry—a beacon of light to ourselves and others. God must have preeminence.

true worship

At the beginning of our spiritual journeys, none of us knows the adventures God has in store. We cannot really comprehend who we are called to be in His

Kingdom. To discover our place, we must seek out wisdom and revelation from God. Without an intimate relationship with Him, we'll never find our way. Our inheritance will pass us by; our future may be something other than what we could have realized.

To move out of our inadequacies and into a significant place in the Kingdom, we must allow the Holy Spirit to work in our lives. The Spirit will help us upgrade our worship, praise and adoration. When we learn to worship in spirit and in truth (as we read in John 4:23–24 Jesus said to the woman of Samaria), we will see ourselves in a way we have never experienced before.

Worship attracts this revelation. When we get into a place of worship, we start to discover things God wants us to know. Scales fall off our eyes, and our minds are renewed. We begin to have dreams, see visions and have thoughts so profound we have to write them down.

> "Worship is God's enjoyment of us and our enjoyment of Him. Worship is a response to the Father/child relationship."
> —Graham Kendrick

In Ephesians 1:17, we read Paul's prayer that the Ephesian Christians would have "the spirit of wisdom and revelation in the knowledge of Him." This knowledge is all about what God wants to be for us. This revelation gives us energy and peace; it overcomes who we are.

When I am overwhelmed, I am always rescued by the same spirit of wisdom and revelation about who God is for me. I get out of the trap of my inadequacy and insecurity by remembering everything He has done for me. In our weakness, He comes and kisses us and calls us again.

gratitude

Gratefulness may be humanity's most underestimated devotional tool. We often forget that gratitude is how we access God's presence. The psalmist sang:

> Enter into His gates with thanksgiving,
> and into His courts with praise.
> Be thankful to Him,
> and bless His name.
> For the LORD is good;
> His mercy is everlasting,
> And His truth endures to all generations.
>
> Psalm 100:4–5

It is always good to set aside a few hours just to be thankful. Make a list of the things you are grateful for. A lack of gratitude can lead us into feeling nothing is happening or into frustration over hassles and issues. In that moment, stop and ask yourself, *What are the benefits in my life right now?*

In the West, we do not know how well-off we truly are. Two-thirds of the world does not eat more than five meals a week. God has blessed us, and it is important that we think about it. I long to see Christians get beyond themselves to start seeing the glory of God as it pertains to their own lives. We need great people who understand that their success is wrapped up in the sovereignty of God.

> "If you concentrate on finding whatever is good in every situation, you will discover that your life will suddenly be filled with gratitude, a feeling that nurtures the soul."
> —Rabbi Harold Kushner

If we can do that, a faith, power, energy and zeal will emerge that will take us forward in the things of the Holy Spirit. We must become overwhelmed with who God wants to be for us.

inheriting the promise

And we desire that each one of you show the same diligence so as to realize the full assurance of hope until the end, so that you will not be sluggish, but imitators of those who through faith and patience inherit the promises. For when God made the promise to Abraham, since He could swear by no one greater, He swore by Himself, saying, "I WILL SURELY BLESS YOU AND I WILL SURELY MULTIPLY YOU." And so, having patiently waited, he obtained the promise. For men swear by one greater than themselves, and with them an oath given as confirmation is an end of every dispute. In the same way God, desiring even more to show to the heirs of the promise the unchangeableness of His purpose, interposed with an oath, so that by two unchangeable things in which it is impossible for God to lie, we who have taken refuge would have strong encouragement to take hold of the hope set before us. This hope we have as an anchor of the soul, a hope both sure and steadfast and one which enters within the veil, where Jesus has entered as a forerunner for us, having become a high priest forever according to the order of Melchizedek.

Hebrews 6:11–20, NASB

At the heart of all God's dealings with us is the issue of our inheritance in Christ. We are the beloved of the Father, the Bride of Christ, people of the Spirit, "not returning evil for evil or insult for insult, but giving a blessing instead; for you were called for the very purpose that you might inherit a blessing" (1 Peter 3:9, NASB).

We are called to inherit. It is what we demonstrate to the earth. We are people of promise. We have hope, an inheritance and a language in which we communicate our confidence in the Father. That language we learn from heaven. The Holy Spirit communicates the heart of the Father in such a powerful way that we are radically changed by the conversation and the content. We then communicate to others in exactly the way we heard it from the Lord—the same intonation, breathless excitement and confidence-boosting manner in which it was delivered to our hearts.

To inherit we need two priceless things, which we receive from God in the process of our circumstances—faith and patience. This is a wonderful contrast, learned only through process. Process is a series of steps designed to achieve a particular goal or learning objective.

Faith speaks about *immediacy*, and patience refers to *eventuality*. Most Christians want the magic Midas touch of instantaneous receiving from the Lord. Faith is a gift to be received but also a disciplined confidence we must learn. We cannot go through life always requiring a gift of faith. God gives gifts as He wills. He wants us to learn how to grow faith, increase in it and walk by it. For this to occur we must attach patience to our faith so that we walk on the path God has provided. Circumstances are often so intense that they seem to last for ages. Primarily this is because we face them in our emotions rather than our wills. The will is the vehicle for faith to attain the will of God.

The promise is secure; God does not lie. The issue is always process. The path of God (process) is always about increasing our confidence, enlarging expectation, learning to stand in peace, being stretched in faith and being schooled in how to see God and hold onto Him. His Word is the anchor point for process to be attained.

What is the gap between the promise and the provision for you in your situation? What is the process designed to fit that space? What is the pathway God has chosen for you to develop greater confidence as well as to receive the provision? Meditate on these things and activate your will toward the Lord. Learn what your current process is all about and how you can cooperate with the Spirit. This is walking by faith.

Faith is confident expectation; patience is calmness and composure. The two combined produce a fortitude and consistency. There is a serene persistence that allows us to keep God in our sights and rejoice in Him. Serene persistence is anathema to doubt, fear and unbelief.

God is unchanging and trustworthy; so is His word. When promising Abraham a son, the Father took an oath in His own name. The oath and God's name are the same. God's name and His nature are equal. Because of who He is, our confident expectation (hope) is anchored in His personality.

God's promises emanate from behind the curtain—the division that separates the Holy Place from the Most Holy Place. This is the place Jesus occupies as our High Priest. He is in God's presence at all times, continuously interceding for us to be all that the Father intends.

Although the promise may sometimes be fulfilled immediately because the Lord may be showing you how to handle a gift of faith, the promise will always be fulfilled, but usually over time through the process of faith.

Give yourself to the Father of lights, from whom every gift is given (see James 1:17). He is the Unchanging One. We see Him best when we are single-minded (focused) about His goodness. Double-minded people are always disappointed and eventually disinherit themselves.

Process is the key to walking by faith. And

combining your faith with patience gives a guarantee of inheritance. Serene persistence – nothing is more precious in a faith lifestyle.

conclusion

The sad truth about many longtime Christians is that they have never understood the magnitude of God's love. Some have served Him for decades and not known His passion for them. But I believe He is going to make up for that lost time. We need to receive this love with a childlike simplicity, not overanalyzing it or trying to strive for it.

God is going to come to us in this next season of time, and His love will be almost beyond our capacity to bear. It will be the stuff of dreams, an unimaginable, monumental, incredible, astonishing, marvelous, outrageous love. This will change the way we think about everything. God's dream for us is that we would be immersed in the majesty of everything He feels for us.

His love will overwhelm us, leading us past logic, reason and intellect into a place where our hearts will be touched as they have never been touched before. This is a season of wonder for us, and we will have to learn to live like much-loved children.

The journey now is to cultivate an expectancy for and to interpret everything in the love of God. God wants to root and ground us in His love so deeply that we live there for the rest of our days. This love will cause us to grow to be the men and women God most wants us to be.

It is exciting to think of how radically this love will change our lives. We will experience the breadth, length, height and depth of God's love for us. His love language will wash over us, again and again.

Love God and love our neighbor—this is our destiny and our honor.

appendix 1

meditation

To meditate means to think deeply about something or someone. It means to explore with mind and heart, allowing what we think to touch our innermost beings.

Meditation is creative thought that leads us to the higher realm of revelation and wisdom. It takes us beyond the place of reason to where joy is seated and faith is activated.

Meditation allows us to search inside and outside the box of our current paradigm. What we see and hear there touches us profoundly. It adds a ring around the core truth of Christ, which is God within, the certainty of freedom.

Fruitful meditation is therefore not a casual seeking for revelatory insight. Initial creative thoughts are merely the X that marks the spot. There is treasure in meditation, a guarantee of wealth in the pursuit of God.

Many are satisfied with collecting random truth on the surface of their consciousness. This is good, wholesome stuff, but it does not satisfy, and it cannot challenge the complexities of life in a warfare context. Deep truth has to be mined over days and weeks. It takes joy and patience to take truth down to its deepest level: beyond meeting our current needs, beyond the depth of understanding the power it releases to us against our adversary, up to the heights where God lives, in the highest places of heaven. For all meditation must ultimately come before the throne of His majesty, sovereignty and supremacy. He fills all things with Himself.

Our situation requires wisdom, but even more it yearns for presence. Meditation allows us to experience both, through the Word coming alive in our spirits. Meditation leads us to God and the permission of His heart. Let the Holy Spirit teach you how to abide. Turn inwardly and rest, wait patiently—He will come. When your heart gets restless, turn to worship. When the interior atmosphere settles, return to listening.

Write down initial thoughts but do not pursue them just yet. Do not be distracted by what you hear initially. Set it aside, and come back to it later.

When first entering a lifestyle of meditation, take care to ease into it slowly: an hour at first, then longer until half a day and so on.

Always have a focus; do not try to wait in a vacuum. In this next exercise is a particular statement, followed by a series of questions. This is both to give you practice in meditation and to bring you into revelation of God through the focus statement.

Use the questions as the Spirit leads. This exercise is not prescriptive but is merely a guide to enable your contemplation. No doubt you will discover better questions as the Holy Spirit tutors you. Enjoy!

appendix 2

"Stand in your problem, holding onto the promise, looking for the provision."

► Engage your heart with the picture this statement provokes.
► What does this mean for you?
► What problems require God's blessing?
► What particular promise is the Holy Spirit drawing to your attention? Ask for scriptural support.
► Study the promise(s). Look for key words and phrases. Write down specifically what the Lord is guaranteeing to you in your current circumstances.

- ► How will you stand and position yourself before the Father?
- ► What level of confidence does the Father wish to bestow on you?
- ► What fear, unbelief and inadequacy must you give up in favor of the promise?
- ► View the promise and the provision together until they fill your vision and hope and faith begin to rise.
- ► Now, through the lens of the promise, look at the problem. What has changed in your
  - – heart
  - – viewpoint
  - – mindset
- ► Compose a prayer before the Lord, a request for His grace, kindness and power to enable you to receive.
- ► Write a psalm of thanksgiving to the Lord for what He has done in and for you in this situation.
- ► Write out in full a confession and a declaration you can speak into your circumstances by the power of the Holy Spirit.
- ► As you challenge your circumstances with your newfound revelation, a boldness and confidence will enter your speech. How did you feel?

► Continue declaring, believing and challenging daily until God speaks further or the problem disappears.
► What has changed in you?
► What have you learned?
► What have you become in Christ?
► Finally, enter all these things in your personal journal. Keep a record of your walk with God in this way, not only to encourage you in later times but also as a legacy to your family and friends.

appendix 3

lectio divina

Lectio Divina (Latin for "Divine Reading") is an ancient way of reading the Bible—allowing a quiet and contemplative way of coming to God's Word. Lectio Divina opens the pulse of the Scripture, helping readers dig far deeper into the Word than normally happens in a quick glance-over.

In this exercise, we will look at a portion of Scripture and use a modified Lectio Divina technique to engage it. This technique can be used on any piece of Scripture; I highly recommend using it for key Bible passages the Lord has highlighted for you and for anything you think might be an inheritance word for your life (see my book *Crafted Prayer* for more on inheritance words).

But now, thus says the LORD, who created you,
O Jacob,
And He who formed you, O Israel:
"Fear not, for I have redeemed you;
I have called you by your name;
You are Mine.
When you pass through the waters, I will be with
you;
And through the rivers, they shall not overflow
you.
When you walk through the fire, you shall not be
burned,
Nor shall the flame scorch you.
For I am the LORD your God,
The Holy One of Israel, your Savior;
I gave Egypt for your ransom,
Ethiopia and Seba in your place.
Since you were precious in My sight,
You have been honored,
And I have loved you;
Therefore I will give men for you,
And people for your life.
Fear not, for I am with you;
I will bring your descendants from the east,
And gather you from the west;
I will say to the north, 'Give them up!'
And to the south, 'Do not keep them back!'

Bring My sons from afar,
And My daughters from the ends of the earth—
Everyone who is called by My name,
Whom I have created for My glory;
I have formed him, yes, I have made him."

Isaiah 43:1-7

1. Find a place of stillness before God. Embrace His peace. Calm your body and breathe slowly— clear your mind of the distractions of life. Ask God to reveal His rest to you. Whisper the word "stillness." This can take some time, but once you are in that place of rest, enjoy it. Worship God out of it.

2. Read the passage twice, slowly.

    a. Allow its words to become familiar to you, to sink into your spirit. Picture the scene and become part of it. Listen for pieces that catch your attention.

    b. Following the reading, meditate upon what you have heard. What stands out? Write it down:

    . . . .
    . . . .
    . . . .
    . . . .
    . . . .

c. If a word or phase from the passage seems highlighted to you, write it down:

. . . .
. . . .
. . . .
. . . .
. . . .
. . . .

3. Read the passage twice again.
   a. Like waves crashing onto a shore, let the words of the text crash onto your spirit. What are you discerning? What are you hearing? What are you feeling? Write it down:

. . . .
. . . .
. . . .
. . . .
. . . .
. . . .

   b. What is the theme of this passage? Write it down:

. . . .
. . . .
. . . .
. . . .
. . . .

c. Does this passage rekindle any memories or experiences? Write them down:

. . . .
. . . .
. . . .
. . . .
. . . .
. . . .

d. What is the Holy Spirit saying to you? Write it down:

. . . .
. . . .
. . . .
. . . .
. . . .
. . . .

4. Read the passage two final times.
   a. Meditate on it.
   b. Is there something God wants you to do with this passage? Is there something He is calling you to? Write it down:

. . . .
. . . .
. . . .
. . . .
. . . .

c. Pray silently. Tell God what this text is
leading you to think about. Ask Him for His
thoughts. Write down your conversation—as
if you and God are sitting in a coffee shop,
two old and dear friends, sharing:

. . . .

. . . .

. . . .

. . . .

. . . .

. . . .

5. Pray and thank God for what He has shared
with you. Come back to the passage a few more
times over the coming weeks.

appendix 4

My beloved one

My beloved one,

Heaven is not bankrupt, and I am not capricious in My giving. I am wholehearted and unchanging in My love for you.

In all of My dealings with you I do seek your growth, an increase in depth and maturity. I stretch out circumstances because I am stretching (increasing) your faith. I am seeking to show you more of how I think and develop you to walk in My paths and know My ways.

Always look to Me. I am the Father who never changes. You are My first fruits to Myself. Everything I do with and for you is by the truth and the exercise of My will.

Live the same as I do. Love the truth and see the will as the primary vehicle for receptivity. Do not allow your emotions to run the show, because they will agitate against faith. Your will cooperates with faith and waits patiently for the promise to be fulfilled.

You were called for the very purpose that you might inherit a blessing. The blessing depends upon your positioning before Me. In all things I am teaching you how to be God conscious in all your ways. Developing your will in submission to Mine increases your stability, enlarges your power and enhances your faith.

There is a difference between being slow and being patient. Your Father is not slow but patiently waits for the right time and the right growth.

As you learn to receive My promises, know that I am wanting you to learn much more than how to obtain things. I am teaching you about position, using the will, learning patience and being stretched.

It is through faith *and* patience that you will inherit the promises. I am wholehearted toward you *within* the process I have designated for you in your current circumstances.

The process is the path. Follow it and find Me. I am not far from you. Walk in the manner I am teaching you. All things always work in your favor. Favor can be immediate or eventual according to the time frame I have set for you in this current phase.

Relax. Rest in Me. I know what is best. Learn the process of how I want to give to you in this current season. Then everything will come to you and all things will fall to you, as I have decreed.

Your Loving Father

appendix 5

Using Psalm 25:1–5 as a foundation for meditation, write your own version of a crafted prayer that fits your current situation and what you are learning about the language of love.

about the author

Graham Cooke is married to Heather, and they have three adult children, Ben, Seth and Sophie. Graham and Heather divide their time between Southampton, England, and Vacaville, California.

Graham is a member of the apostolic team of c.net (Cornerstone), a network of ministries and a family of churches spanning 44 nations. He is a member of Community Church in Southampton (UK), responsible for the prophetic and training program, and works with team leader Billy Kennedy. In California, he is part of the pastoral leadership team and works with senior pastor David Crone. He has responsibility for Insight, a training program within the church and for the region.

Graham, a popular conference speaker, is well-known for his training programs on the prophetic, spiritual warfare, intimacy with God, leadership and spirituality. He functions as a consultant within c.net (and beyond), specifically helping churches make the transition from one dimension of calling to a higher level of vision and ministry. He has a passion to build prototype churches that can fully reach our postmodern society.

A strong part of Graham's ministry is in producing finances and resources to help the poor, and he supports many projects around the world. He also financially supports and helps to underwrite church planting, leadership development, evangelism and health and rescue projects in the developing world. If you wish to become a financial partner for the sake of missions, please contact Graham's office, where his personal assistant, Carole Shiers, will be able to assist you.

Graham has many prayer partners who play a significant part in his ministry. For more information, check his website (below).

Graham has written four other books, *Developing Your Prophetic Gifting* (Chosen), *A Divine Confrontation ... Birth Pangs of the New Church* (Destiny Image), *Crafted Prayer* (Chosen) and *The Secret of a Powerful Inner Life* (Chosen).

You can learn more about Graham Cooke at:

Graham Cooke
P.O. Box 91
Southampton
SO15 5ZE
United Kingdom

Website: www.grahamcooke.com